Intermittent Fasting and You

Intermittent Fasting and You

Carol Lowe

RESOURCE *Publications* • Eugene, Oregon

Contents

Intermittent Fasting and You

Congratulations on thinking about, taking the first steps, or reinventing your journey to a healthier, happier you. I know it's hard, and we've all done this and failed—perhaps too many times to count. But this time will be different! This time we are going to rely solely on our Savior and King Jesus Christ's strength to conquer this goal. Whether you are trying to lose 5, 10, 20, 60, 100 pounds or more, the Lord will be here with you every step of the way. My goal is to lose 70 pounds. In Mark 10:27, Jesus tells us, "With men it is impossible, but not with God; for with God all things are possible." Matthew 17:20 states, "I say to you, if you have faith as a mustard seed, you will say to this mountain, 'Move from here to there,' and it will move; and nothing will be impossible for you." My mountain is excess fat and cellulite. So, say it out loud with me: "MOVE, MOUNTAIN! Move from my stomach and thighs! Move from my back and my arms! Move from my chin and my ankles! Move from my hips and booty! MOVE, MOUNTAIN!"

At day 39 of my intermittent fasting journey, I had lost 22 pounds, weighed 232 pounds, and had a body mass index (BMI) of 31.1. I have no doubts that the Lord will see me to my 70-pound goal so that I may glorify him with my transformation. The Lord will bring me through, so that he and I can partner together in order for others to glorify him with their healthier lifestyles. Together, the three of us can bring his kingdom agenda to all who see his glory through us.

I know you may be wondering, exactly what is intermittent fasting? Fasting has been apart of the Christian lifestyle as a way to tune out the world and tune into God. Fasting from food or other things that hold our attention or focus allows us to be filled with Christ instead. Jesus said in Luke 4:4, "It is written, 'Man shall not live by bread alone, but by every word of God.'" Fasting is a wonderful tool to strengthen our relationship with God. It was not until recently that we started to understand the health benefits of fasting as well. This brings us to intermittent fasting.

Intermittent fasting (IF), also known as intermittent energy restriction, is an umbrella term for various meal timing schedules that cycle between voluntary fasting and non-fasting over a given period. Three methods of intermittent fasting are alternate-day fasting, periodic fasting, and daily time-restricted feeding. Simply put, it's an eating pattern that rotates between periods of fasting and eating. I've been using the daily time-restricted feeding. I fast for twenty hours and have a four-hour eating window. No, I don't eat for the entire four hours, and neither will you. The best part is that IF doesn't require restrictive dieting. You would eat as normal. It's not so much about what you eat but when you eat. Simply making smarter choices with portion sizes and staying away from overly fatty foods is all the dieting you'll need to do. As we are serious about living healthier, this is something we are prepared to do from the start.

Psalm 139:14 states that we are all "fearfully and wonderfully made." No matter our weight, size, or looks, the Lord loves us all. He is more concerned about our hearts than our appearance. First Samuel 16:7 states, "But the LORD said to Samuel, 'Do not look at his appearance or at his physical stature, because I have refused him. For the LORD does not see as man sees; for man looks at the outward appearance, but the LORD looks at the heart.'" Intermittent fasting is not just about not eating to drop pounds in order to fit into your skinny clothes. Getting skinny will not conquer your battle with food. We've proven that over and over again. Intermittent fasting can assist us in filling up on God instead of empty calories and sugar. We have been trying to sustain a spiritual craving and hunger with physical nourishment. This has left our spirits malnourished and our bodies in a state of perpetual obesity. Intermittent fasting can help us flip the script and let our spirits feast on the buffet of our King and finally be satisfied.

My IF journey has been absolutely amazing! I have been able to create the fasting times that work best for me and my family. You will be able to do the same for maximum results. My fast window is from 8:00 p.m. to 4:00 p.m and my eating window is from 4:00 p.m. to 8:00 p.m. each day. During those times, I am free from the burden of wondering what I should eat, how much I should eat, how many calories I have had, how long the food will sustain me before I'm hungry again. I am finally free from the pull and power of food, the constant cravings, the overeating and self-loathing. I am no longer a slave to desserts, large portions of pasta, and fried foods. The Lord, in his infinite knowledge, has set me free. Now that I am free, I want to help you allow God to break your chains of bondage. I hope you will join me on this journey!

First Things First

BEFORE WE BEGIN, I want to urge you to accept the free gift of salvation. When Adam accepted the forbidden fruit from Eve and ate—in what is known as the fall—he plunged the whole world into sin. Every molecule on the earth was cursed with sin. Every person to ever live would be born with a sinful nature. We sin without trying and without ceasing. First John 1:8–10 tells us, "If we say that we have no sin, we deceive ourselves, and the truth is not in us. If we confess our sins, He is faithful and just to forgive us our sins and to cleanse us from all unrighteousness. If we say that we have not sinned, we make Him a liar, and His word is not in us." We are doomed to a life and death separated from God.

We need to be saved but we cannot save ourselves. After disobeying God, Adam and Eve realized they were naked and tried to cover themselves. They tried to save themselves from the shame of their nakedness. Now, people are still trying to cover the shame and stench of their sin by spending hours at church, giving to charitable foundations and living good, Christian lives. These things are nice, but they will not save your soul from eternal separation from God. If we could save ourselves with works, there would be no reason for Christ's death.

Romans 6:23 tells us, "For the wages of sin is death, but the gift of God is eternal life in Christ Jesus our Lord." God is holy and righteous; he cannot allow the price of sin to go unpaid. Thankfully, he is also merciful and gracious. He loved us all so much, he made a way for our sin to be paid in full. He has provided us with a perfect covering, so that we can have intimacy with him and spend eternity in his wonderful kingdom. John 3:16–17 says, "For God so loved the world that He gave His only begotten Son, that whoever believes in Him should not perish but have everlasting life. For God did not send His Son into the world to condemn the world, but that the world through Him might be saved." Jesus's brutal death on the cross paid the balance for every person's sin. When we believe in him and accept him into our hearts, we are covered with his purity, righteousness, and sanctification. Praise God! If you have not accepted Christ as your personal Lord and Savior, please do so now. Don't waste another second in the shameful nakedness of your inherited sin!

Prayer

Dear Heavenly Father, I am a sinner. I have sinned and will continue to sin as long as you allow me to live. I am a vile creature in the midst of your perfect glory. I am undeserving and wretched. I need you. I love you because you first loved me. I believe that your Son died on the cross to save my life. His death paid the price for all of my sin. Cleanse me with his blood and let your beautiful Holy Spirit guide my life so that you can use me to advance your kingdom. In Jesus's holy name, I pray. Amen.

Idolatry

Like many people, I have been battling with my weight and self-image for most of my adult life. I spent my youth participating in year-round athletics and played a few years of collegiate Division 1 basketball. I was very active, and my body reflected my activity. But after quitting the team after two disappointing seasons and going through six pitiful academic semesters, filled with excessive drinking and greasy take-out, I was almost completely unrecognizable. I had ballooned from 180 pounds to 260 pounds, and I felt terrible.

I have gained and lost weight repeatedly over the years. Losing weight always meant hours of exercise, running, sweat, squats, all types of lunges, unseasoned food, salads, and hunger. I would literally work my butt off but be unable to keep it off. I would always gain back everything I lost, plus more. I carried the feeling of disgust and defeat around with me everywhere. They say that nothing tastes as good as being skinny feels, and they're right. No one thing does; but comfort foods, sugary drinks, busy schedules, guilty pleasures, and/or lounging around from being run down by life make it hard to care about being skinny. When you're surviving day to day, whether it be raising kids, working a demanding job or multiple jobs, taking care of aging parents, or being married, being healthy and taking care of yourself always seems to take a back seat.

After having my second daughter, I desperately wanted to get healthy. I wanted to be able to teach my girls how to be fit. I didn't want them spending their lives yo-yo dieting and dealing with weight issues. I didn't want my inner voice of inadequacy, self-disgust, and nitpicking to become their inner voices. I wanted to change but did not know where to begin.

My girls are very spoiled, and we spend every minute of the day together. Taking off to spend one to two hours at the gym was not an option. To be honest, I wasn't too sad about that, because the gym has skinny people, being cute in their skinny workout clothes, not breathing heavy and looking gross, like I knew I would have looked. Spending a few hours alone at home, working out uninterrupted, was completely out of the question, too. I don't know about yours, but my kids know nothing of personal space, privacy, or alone time. Months passed by, and I was no closer to becoming any healthier. In fact, the numbers on the scale were getting bigger and bigger. I was in trouble, but my God came through and showed me the way. "Ask, and it will be given to you; seek, and you will find; knock, and it will be opened to you" (Matt 7:7).

It was during a sermon given by my beloved preacher and uncle, Michael Lowe, at my home church, Grace Bible Baptist, that the Lord made everything clear to me. Michael was speaking on idolatry—hang with me, this will all make sense, I promise. The dictionary has the meaning of idolatry as the worship of idols. It's listed as the extreme admiration, love, or reverence for something or someone. For us Christians, idolatry would mean serving gods other than the one true God. God is very clear on his stance about idolatry. In Exod 20:3, God tells us, "You shall have no other gods before Me." God despises idolatry. He is the one, true God, and he will not accept sharing his rightly deserved worship with anyone or anything else. Michael explained that "idolatry was when we looked to any noun, person, place, or thing to meet our needs, or who or what we look to for guidance or comfort over God. Anything we put before God and his will can be made into a idol." He asked that we ask ourselves honestly what we run to in times of distress, anger, sadness, joy, boredom, and confusion. I looked honestly and could provide no other answer than my yummy food; I was serving my stomach and didn't even know. My weight, jiggling rolls of fat, and cellulite were all evidence that I could not refute. Romans 16:18 states, "For those who are such do not serve our Lord Jesus Christ, but their own belly."

If I'm having a hard day or I am sad, I want something yummy to comfort me. When I'm celebrating, I want to enjoy a nice meal. I can remember snacking incessantly, for no reason, on lazy Saturdays (before my girls arrived—lazy Saturday, ha!). I have a happy dance reserved for moments when my food is especially tasty or when I get to enjoy that for which I have a specific craving. I do not have a dance reserved for God.

Matthew 6:24 states, "No one can serve two masters; for either he will hate the one and love the other, or else he will be loyal to the one and despise the other. You cannot serve God and mammon." I love God. He is amazing, but I have spent my entire Christian life loving him second to my stomach. My stomach has always been my spouse; my poor Savior, my side piece. I go to God in times of distress and joy, just after I've fed my stomach. If my stomach wants tacos, it will get tacos, by any means necessary. If it's 2:00 in the morning and my stomach wants a yummy snacky snack, a yummy snacky snack it shall get. Let God instruct me or tell me to do something, and I will either find a reason not to do it or a reason why it can be done at a later date. Despicable! That was a truth that I could not live another second accepting. It was time for an immediate change!

If you can relate to food as I do, please take the time to acknowledge your idolatry and ask God for forgiveness. There is no shame in admitting this. Now that we know, we can ask our Father to help us fix it.

Prayer

Dear Heavenly Father, as I now realize my idolatrous behavior with food and my stomach, I ask you in your infinite mercy to forgive me. I have treated you ignorantly and carelessly and have not held you in the holy esteem that you so richly deserve. You are my God, my only God! Reveal to me other idols in my life that threaten my relationship with you. Help me to banish them from my life. You are the creator of the heavens and earth. I will praise you always. "Holy, holy, holy is the Lord God Almighty, who was, and is, and is to come." "You are worthy, our Lord and God, to receive glory and honor and power, for you created all things, and by your will they were created and have their being." Thank you for loving me despite my shortcomings, and help me to love you in all of Your magnificence. In Jesus's holy name, amen.

The Basics of Intermittent Fasting

ALTHOUGH THIS REVELATION shook me to my core, I still was not sure how to proceed. So I prayed and fasted for guidance. One late night, after being awakened by one of my daughters, I was unable to fall back to sleep. I prayed and started playing a word search game to get my eyes feeling heavy. It was after a game that an ad for *Fastic*, an intermittent fasting app, played. It piqued my interest, and I downloaded it and read the information. There was God, showing me the way. "Call to Me, and I will answer you, and show you great and mighty things, which you do not know" (Jer 33:3).

The *Fastic* app was amazing. It was informative, kept up with my water intake, fasting hours, weight, BMI, and step counter. The app also had helpful tips and information. I'd hit the proverbial jackpot!

Fastic explained IF and helped me understand how intermittent fasting worked with my body to shed the pounds. I was able to understand, in simple language, what happens to my body during the fasts.

The body begins to digest food immediately after food is consumed and begins processing carbohydrates. Carbohydrates or carbs are essential nutrients that are found in many foods like bread, beans, milk, popcorn, potatoes, cookies, spaghetti, soft drinks, corn, and pie. They also come in many forms, the most common being fiber, starches, and sugars. Carbohydrates are processed and released into the bloodstream as glucose or sugar, causing the rise in blood sugar levels. This rise in blood sugar levels causes the body to produce an important hormone, insulin. The production of insulin is vital, as it promotes the tissues intake of the glucose, which supplies the body with energy.

Insulin also stores energy. During meals, the body is typically overloaded with more carbs or sugar than is needed. When the body has extra glucose, it is stored in liver and muscles. Stored glucose is called glycogen. Glycogen is the body's backup fuel and is released back into the bloodstream when the body needs a quick energy boost or when a person's blood sugar level drops. When the glycogen storages are full, the excess glycogen becomes fat. This is why it is so important not to overeat, and this is why fasting is so imperative to our health. It allows the body to use up all of its energy reserve and burn away the fat that is stored around our stomachs, buttocks, and backs.

Blood sugar levels in the body typically drop three hours after the consumption of the last meal. This drop is caused by insulin moving glucose from the blood to the tissues. During this process, fat is not used as a primary energy source. The body will start using fat for energy once both the glucose and glycogen are drained.

The blood sugar levels in the body even out around nine hours after the last meal. The body takes a quick break when digestion is complete and the production of insulin ceases. Once the blood sugar levels drop, the hormone glycagon is engaged. Glycagon takes the glycogen from the tissues and puts it back into the bloodstream. This process maintains sugar levels and energy distribution in the body.

The body is constantly using energy, and the process of moving glucose from the bloodstream to the muscles and back is never ending. Once the glucose is depleted, the body will start to use the largest source of energy, the fat reserves. The body will tap into the fat reserves around eleven hours after the last meal is eaten.

Fastic states the following regarding the fasting process:[1]

> The average calorie supply of an adult person in the form
> of fat reserves amounts to about 80,000 calories.

---

1. *Fastic: Fasting App.*

In order to tap into these reserves, your body starts producing fat-burning hormones. An impressive six hormones, listed below, are involved in this vital mechanism. These hormones perform more or less the same function for fat metabolism:

- Growth Hormones (Human Growth Hormone, HGH)

- IGF-1 (Insulin like Growth Factor)

- Glucagon

- Testosterone

- Adrenaline

- T3 (triiodothyronine)

The body starts to produce ketone bodies or ketones in conjunction with the process of fat burning. This happens twelve hours after the consumption of the last meal. Ketones are formed when the fat reserves in the body are broken down. Ketones provide energy to the heart and brain, which is why focus and productivity are increased during fasting.

The best phase, in my opinion, happens fourteen hours after the last meal is eaten. When there is no food intake for over twelve hours and after the conversion to fat metabolism, autophagy is activated.

Fastic states the following to explain autophagy:[2]

An interesting word with an even more fascinating function. Autophagy, translated from the Greek autophagos, which means "to consume oneself." And this is exactly what happens during autophagy. Your cells begin to process "themselves."

Old cell components and so-called "misfiled" proteins are recycled, but cells can be completely renewed.

So your body is undergoing a big clear out and proper clean up. This not only makes your cells more efficient,

2. *Fastic: Fasting App.*

it also prolongs the life of your cells and with that your own.

During this phase, your body is literally eating itself. This knowledge is constantly in the back of my mind. More times than not, knowing that I will enter autophagy soon or knowing that I am in this state will help me stick to my fasting goal. I see adorable Pac-Man characters chomping away at my unsightly pockets of cellulite and folds of rolls that jiggle when I move.

I don't know about you, but I had no clue all this happened to our bodies while we fasted. This knowledge puts a entirely new spin on Ps 51:10: "Create in me a clean heart, O God, and renew a steadfast spirit within me." When we strive to be close to God with fasting, he is renewing both our spirits and bodies.

When we deny our primal instincts to eat in an attempt to strengthen our relationship with God, we truly gain so much more in return. Fasting seems so in line with the simple beauty of our King—just like the way he has made for us to receive salvation. We need only believe that he is God and that his Son paid the price for our sin. Jesus says in John 5:24, "Most assuredly, I say to you, he who hears My word and believes in Him who sent Me has everlasting life, and shall not come into judgment, but has passed from death into life."

Getting Started

Now that you have some information on intermittent fasting, we can discuss how to get started. I've found that in all new challenges, phases, and journeys, it's always best to pray first.

Prayer

> *Dear Heavenly Father, thank you for opening my eyes to my idolatrous behavior with food and my stomach. Thank you for providing a way for me to be free from this sin and the bondage that has had such a negative impact on my life. Guide my steps and decisions as I embark on this journey to become healthier. Keep my eyes, mind, and heart on you for strength, as I know this will not be easy, but it will be worth it! I know that your Holy Spirit is flowing through me, so that I can never forget that you are my Savior in all things and in every area of my life. I love you, and I am truly grateful for this opportunity. Thank you for never giving up on me. Help me to quiet the voices of previous failures and missteps that tell me that I am not worthy of this change. Help me to see me as you see me. Forgive my unbelief and fill my heart with endless encouragement. In Jesus's name, I pray, amen!*

Before we begin, take a current inventory of your weight, BMI, and body measurements. Everyone loses weight differently and in different areas first. Knowing from where you start makes where you'll end even sweeter. The numbers don't lie.

The *Fastic* app offers twelve intermittent fasting plans:[1]

> The first number in the sequence is the number of hours fasting; the second number is the number of hours in the eating window.
>
> Starter: 12:12, 13:11, 14:10, 15:9
>
> Advanced: 16:8, 17:7, 18:6, 19:5
>
> Professional: 20:4, 21:3, 22:2, 23:1

I would recommend starting where you feel most comfortable. Be honest with yourself and avoid selecting a plan that you will not realistically be able to sustain. Doing so will only frustrate you and threaten to stop this process before you even get started. Again, I started with 20:4, as fasting had already been a part of my walk with Christ.

Once you have selected your plan, you will need to decide the time frames for your fasting and eating windows. Take your time with this part, because it is vital to your success. Think about a normal week for you. When are you your busiest or hungriest? What times are you available to connect with God in prayer or Bible reading or devotional readings? My fasting window is from 8:00 p.m. to 4:00 p.m. This works especially well for me because I'm in bed by 9:30 p.m., so the majority of my fasting is spent when I'm asleep or trying to sleep. It's also great because I don't have to struggle to find time to eat during the day. Easy-peasy!

The next step is to get active. Most of us already own a Fitbit, Apple watch, wrist pedometer or have a step counter on our smart phones. It's time to dust them off and use them. Before starting this journey, I thought I was very active. I mean, I spent my days chasing around my extremely active girls who go nonstop all day. Clearly, I was in denial, as I did not have the body of an active person. It's for this reason that I would suggest spending your first IF day taking stock of your normal amount of activity. This way you will be able to see your exact activity range.

---

1. *Fastic: Fasting App.*

The Ten Thousand Steps Organization states:

> Low activity is 5,000 to 7,499 steps per day. The somewhat active take between 7,500 to 9,999 steps per day. Active people take more than 10,000 steps per day. Highly active people take more than 12,500.

Whatever your current daily total is, take reasonable steps to get to 10,000 or more steps a day.[2] Walking is a great low-intensity activity to get your body moving. Walking is also a great way to get out in nature and take stock of the beauty that surrounds us. In nature, we see God's glory. He's a true artist, and his work can be breathtaking. On my walks, I feel so connected with him. I feel free to talk to him, pray, cry or just be in a state of gratitude. The Lord that made all we see also crafted each of us in his own image. Our God is truly amazing.

I also recommend locating an IF buddy for fasting and walking. Change is hard. It's always helpful to have someone who's going through the same things as us. Knowing that you're not alone in this process can be very helpful. My aunt Brenda and I have been on this journey together, and I can honestly say that I could not have done this without her. She pushes me every day, and I am so thankful for her.

My mother, Linda, my girls, and our dog walk every morning. I've really enjoyed starting my day being active. As we know, activity breeds activity. We are literal examples of Newton's law of inertia, that objects in motion tend to stay in motion. The more you move, the more you want to move.

I especially enjoy those rare occurrences when my mother and I get to walk alone. She has been a huge supporter of my IF journey, and it's nice to just simply be in her presence and talk. I think this simple act of walking together has been more therapeutic to our relationship than either of us could have ever imagined. I'm thankful for this opportunity to not only heal the damage I've done to my body but heal the damage to our relationship.

2. "Counting Your Steps."

If you do get the opportunity to walk outdoors, please exercise caution and safety. Below are tips to help keep you safe while you walk.

1. Always wear a safety vest or brightly colored clothing.

2. Try to avoid walking at night.

3. Try to walk with someone, whenever possible.

4. Avoid walking on busy or curvy roads.

5. Make sure you stay hydrated.

6. Be sure to tell someone where you plan to walk and when you plan to return.

7. Stay alert at all times.

8. Avoid using headphones that will distort the sounds around you.

9. Use stable surfaces.

10. Carry your ID and emergency contact information with you.

11. If you walk at night, wear reflective clothing and be sure to have a light source.

12. Wear proper shoes.

13. Always walk facing oncoming traffic.

Lastly, I would also recommend starting a fasting journal. Go ahead and have your first entry be your IF goals. How much weight do you want to lose, and what are your spiritual goals? Include your questions and concerns. Again, be honest with yourself! I use my journey journal for everything: how I'm feeling, a Bible verse that spoke to me that day, how the girls were behaving, things I want to pray about, what I ate and why, what I didn't eat and why. The list goes on and on.

All right! Now, we just need to start. Please fight the urge to gorge on food prior to your fasting. I am all too familiar with the Night before Belly Bender (a term brilliantly coined by my Sissy,

Jessica Kuebuafor). Let's go ahead and start our new lifestyle in a different way and with a different mindset.

Ecclesiastes 3:1–8 states, "To everything there is a season, a time for every purpose under heaven: a time to be born, and a time to die; a time to plant, and a time to pluck what is planted; a time to kill, and a time to heal; a time to break down, and a time to build up; a time to weep, and a time to laugh; a time to mourn, and a time to dance; a time to cast away stones, and a time to gather stones; a time to embrace, and a time to refrain from embracing; a time to gain, and a time to lose; a time to keep, and a time to throw away; a time to tear, and a time to sew; a time to keep silence, and a time to speak; a time to love, and a time to hate; a time of war, and a time of peace."

It's time to get started!

The Fat

I AM STILL considered obese after fifty-one days and twenty-five pounds lost, with a BMI of 30.7, but not for much longer. I have dropped four dress sizes. My stomach, arms, legs, and face are noticeably smaller, and I'm finally back to only one chin. I have accrued 1,030 fasting hours on the 20:4 fasting plan while walking at least 12,000 steps a day. Feeling and looking awesome, loving this IF journey!

Twenty-five pounds may not seem like a lot to you. That's probably because you've never picked up my sixteen-month-old daughter and attempted to carry her for any length of time. Trust me, it's substantial, and I couldn't be more pleased with my progress. Maybe you've lost more or less than twenty-five pounds at your fifty-one-day marker. Either way, you're doing an amazing job! Stick with it.

The *U.S. News and World Report* states that the US obesity rate topped 40% in 2020.[1] That is a staggeringly sad number. Americans are literally eating themselves to death.

The CDC states that weight that is higher than what is considered as a healthy weight for a given height is described as overweight or obese. A person is considered obese if he or she has a BMI of 30.0 or higher. People who are overweight or obese are at higher risk for chronic conditions, such as high blood pressure, diabetes, and high cholesterol.[2]

1. Galvin, "US Obesity Rate."

2. Centers for Disease Control and Prevention. "Defining Adult Overweight."

The *Fastic* app states that it is generally known that being overweight is unhealthy and increases the risk of various diseases. However, the location of the excess fat is decisive for the assessment of the risk.[3]

> In general, a distinction can be made between subcutaneous and visceral fat. Subcutaneous fat, as the name suggests is located under the skin and accumulates primarily in the hips, legs and pelvic area. It is rather passive tissue, which serves as energy storage, heat insulation and mechanical protection.
>
> Visceral fat is the abdominal fat that surrounds the internal organs. In contrast to subcutaneous fat, it's hormonal activity is quite high. This is why the probability of suffering from diseases such as type 2 diabetes, cardiovascular diseases, stroke or metabolic syndrome increases significantly with the increase of abdominal girth. Why some people store more of this more harmful fat is still not yet fully understood. It is assumed that hormonal disturbances and stress play a role.
>
> To truly understand, it is necessary to gauge what type of fat is present in the body and where the fat lies, in addition to doing tests to discover imbalances in hormones and quantify stress levels. Therefore, the BMI, which gives results from height and weight, is hardly suitable as a measure of health. Athletic people who have an especially high proportion of heavy muscle mass are often in the overweight range according to this calculation. Instead you should measure your abdominal girth to assess certain health risks. Women with an abdominal girth of more than 94 cm are assumed to have an increased risk of disease. If the abdominal girth is over 88 cm for women and over 102 cm for men, the risk is increased even more. In order to determine the exact amount of visceral fat, only imaging diagnostics, will be able to tell.
>
> The good news—usually the visceral fat is what's broken down first when slimming begins. Do not solely try to orient yourself by the scales, but also by your

3. *Fastic: Fasting App.*

belly circumference. This is best measured before the first meal, at the level of the navel.

I am living proof that the visceral fat goes first. My stomach, hips and legs are much smaller. My shorts are falling off of me. Honestly, this slimming has been the most inspirational and motivating part of this journey for me. It's working. Praise God, it's working!

"You have turned for me my mourning into dancing; You have put off my sackcloth and clothed me with gladness, to the end that my glory may sing praise to You and not be silent. O LORD my God, I will give thanks to You forever" (Ps 30:11–12).

Dependency

THE BEAUTIFUL THING about IF is not just the health benefits but the spiritual benefits. As you know, fasting is a way to deny ourselves food and/or other things that distract us, while allowing us to feast on the things of God (his word, his will, and his kingdom). "'Now, therefore,' says the LORD, 'Turn to Me with all your heart, with fasting, with weeping, and with mourning" (Joel 2:12).

In order to fast, I have needed to depend on God for strength. When hunger pangs hit, he's the only thing that can fill me. Ephesians 3:19 says "to know the love of Christ which passes knowledge; that you may be filled with all the fullness of God."

Reading or listening to the Bible or devotionals not only takes my mind off my current situation but actually feeds my soul. This feeding of my soul has impacted my life in so many powerful ways already. I have to seek God hourly, minute by minute, to help me through the day. Fasting is hard, but my God is there with me always. Zephaniah 3:17 tells us, "The LORD your God in your midst, the Mighty One, will save; He will rejoice over you with gladness, He will quiet you with His love, He will rejoice over you with singing."

There are days when I am exhausted and cannot see how I will be able to reach my step goal. I can't tell you how many days it has felt like the good Lord was moving my feet for me. Or when it's felt like 500 degrees outside, and just when I feel like throwing in the towel, a cool breeze rejuvenates me. It's in those times that I'm truly amazed and thankful by and for him. I cannot do anything without Christ. He is my strength in all things. I am reminded of

Isa 40:30–31, "Even the youths shall faint and be weary, and the young men shall utterly fall, but those who wait on the LORD shall renew their strength; they shall mount up with wings like eagles, they shall run and not be weary, they shall walk and not faint." Praise God!

This new dependency has carried over to every part of my life. I am currently in the midst of a custody battle for my oldest daughter. This battle has shaken every part of me and has affected my entire family. I am terrified and overwhelmed. Thoughts of worst-case scenarios bombard my mind, and my heart cycles between broken and breaking. Without God, I would be paralyzed by this intense fear and the constant what ifs. I find peace in 2 Tim 1:7, "For God has not given us a spirit of fear, but of power and of love and of a sound mind."

Through this fasting journey, the Lord has proven time and time again that he is always with me. When I need him, he will rescue me. That's something that fasting has not only taught my brain but shown my heart. My relationship with God is growing stronger and more substantial.

We all experience troubles that threaten to overtake us. You may be dealing with a personal health crisis, failing health of a loved one, financial crisis, or displacement. I urge you to take your burdens to God. Seek out his will through his word. He never gives us more than we can bear, even if it feels like we're drowning. Take solace in the fact that our God walks on water. He not only walks on water, but he created the water. There is nothing he cannot do. "Now in the fourth watch of the night Jesus went to them, walking on the sea. And when the disciples saw Him walking on the sea, they were troubled, saying, 'It is a ghost!' And they cried out for fear. But immediately Jesus spoke to them, saying, 'Be of good cheer! It is I; do not be afraid'" (Matt 14:25–27).

Although I know IF is going to help all of us lose our desired weight, I hope that you don't miss out on gaining a more intimate relationship with the one true God. Resist the instinct to focus on the temporal and strive to seek the everlasting, eternal goodness and will of our heavenly Father. "But seek first the kingdom of God and His righteousness, and all these things shall be added to you" (Matt 6:33).

Deliverance

"I sought the LORD, and He heard me, and delivered me from all my fears." (Ps 34:4)

My King has delivered me and saved my daughter! On July 23, 2020, I was awarded full custody of my oldest daughter and her father—by DNA only—was denied all visitation. I'm still in shock, and part of me will probably always be in shock.

My attorney, the esteemed Wayne Hollowell, had been telling me for months, that even though he had established no relationship with my daughter, her father would, more than likely, receive visitation. I was sick, thinking of having to send her with a stranger. I'd lost sleep over how this would affect her and affect our relationship. I'd had nightmares about her crying hysterically upon being forced into a car with him and driven off with her screaming for me. I had been brought to my knees by the thoughts of all the things someone who doesn't care about my daughter can do to harm her—physically, emotionally and mentally. That experience was torturous, and I wouldn't wish it on anyone. As the court date approached, I began clinging desperately to God. Tony Evans has a saying that perfectly sums up that final week: "You find out God is all you need when you realize, God is all you have." God was the only person who could deliver us.

Devotionals and daily Scripture reading were the only things keeping me going. The final week, almost every reading was about King Jehoshaphat. Until then, sadly, I had never heard of this particular king. I can tell you that today, 2 Chron 20 is one of my favorite chapters. I urge you to read through this chapter and keep it close when you need to be reminded of God's delivering power.

In this chapter, King Jehoshaphat, ruler of Judah, is under attack from the Moabites, Ammonites, and other unnamed enemies. Upon receiving this knowledge, the king issues a fast throughout the lands of Judah and Jerusalem, as his armies are no match for the approaching onslaught. He brings his kingdom together to praise God and seek guidance. During the gathering of the people, Jahaziel is given the Spirit of the Lord and instructs them that this is God's fight and that God will handle everything; they need only believe. Instead of fighting the enemy on the day of battle, the king orders singers to go before the army to sing praises. Once they begin singing, the Lord causes the enemy armies to start fighting themselves until all are defeated. God did precisely what he said he would do and delivered his people from certain annihilation.

Just like us, Judah and the inhabitants of Jerusalem were under attack. The people of Moab, Ammon, and Seir were attacking Judah's way of life. They were threatening their lives and freedom. Judah was no match for their armies; and there was no way we would leave that courtroom without the father being awarded visitation.

The more I read this chapter, the more assured I became. I could feel God's presence telling me that he would handle everything; I need only believe. The beautiful thing about this chapter is its instructional properties. It's practically a divine playbook on how to handle a crisis.

It tells us that, upon being informed of the attack, King Jehoshaphat sought the Lord. "And Jehoshaphat feared, and set himself to seek the LORD, and proclaimed a fast throughout all Judah" (2 Chron 20:3). He didn't consult his army leaders or walllow in his fear. He went straight to God. Then we see another biblical example of fasting. King Jehoshaphat understood the importance of fasting and used it wisely. Like Jehoshaphat, both my immediate and church families fasted. The last week, my families were on a twenty-four-hour liquid fast. For me, this meant that I had liquids during my four-hour eating window, instead of food.

Next, Jehoshaphat gave God the most amazing pep talk ever recorded. Of course, we know that our King needs no pep talk to perform miracles or save us. He created the heavens and earth with his mighty words. However, his lordship is worthy of all acknowledgment, accolades, and praise. Letting the King know that we understand his power and status shows our humility and dependence. Doing this each day had a profound effect on me. Focusing and reiterating God's character made me focus more on him and his magnificence rather than on my problem and fears.

Jehoshaphat then told the Lord his problem. He acknowledged the vulnerability of his kingdom and expressed that God was the only path for deliverance. He took his problem straight to God. When we take our problems to God, they're no longer ours but God's problem. "Call upon Me in the day of trouble; I will deliver you, and you shall glorify Me" (Ps 50:15). And we all know, there's no problem that God can't solve.

After seeking the Lord, Jehoshaphat and Judah waited for God's instructions. They didn't seek their own deliverance or try to help God, like we often times do. Once receiving word from God, they immediately worshiped him. They all began singing praises to God. They praised him for hearing their cries, for being righteous, and for their upcoming deliverance. Tony Evans states that you can worship God anytime, but praise is public. Praise is an outward show of worship and affection. My family and I began setting aside time each day to openly praise God for his upcoming deliverance. I began sending out daily texts to people, declaring the awesomeness of my God. This open praise of our King is something that we will continue daily from now on.

On the day of battle, King Jehoshaphat reassured his people. He urged them to just believe. To show their faith in God, Jehoshaphat sent out choir members to sing praises to God ahead of his army. He 100% believed that the battle had already been won. "And when he had consulted with the people, he appointed those who should sing to the LORD, and who should praise the beauty of holiness, as they went out before the army and were saying: 'Praise the LORD, for His mercy endures forever'" (2 Chron 20:21).

God does not operate according to this world or our thinking. In the heat of battle against a powerful opponent, you would bring out all of your heavy artillery. Isaiah 55:8–9 (NLT) tells us, "'My thoughts are nothing like your thoughts,' says the Lord. 'And my ways are far beyond anything you could imagine. For just as the heavens are higher than the earth, so my ways are higher than your ways and my thoughts higher than your thoughts.'" God doesn't need our help. When we trust and relinquish control to God in our weakness and trials, his glory and divinity shine through. That's how we usher in his kingdom. Paul states in regards to his physical affliction, "Concerning this thing I pleaded with the Lord three times that it might depart from me. And He said to me, 'My grace is sufficient for you, for My strength is made perfect in weakness.' Therefore most gladly I will rather boast in my infirmities, that the power of Christ may rest upon me. Therefore I take pleasure in infirmities, in reproaches, in needs, in persecutions, in distresses, for Christ's sake. For when I am weak, then I am strong" (2 Cor 12:8–10).

Their faith in the midst of this great trial is truly inspirational. The Lord told them to go to the wilderness to see his victory and they went. Too many times we forget that these are real people in the Bible verses we read. There was an enormous army coming to dismantle their entire lives. In this context, I wouldn't blame any of them for not wanting to show up armed only with hymns and choir boys. The fact that they showed up is amazing in itself.

I remember the fear and feeling of dread that befell me when I left my home for court. I kissed my girls goodbye and became overwhelmed that there was a strong possibility of our way of life and security changing forever upon my return. As I fought back tears and forced out a smile to wave to my girls, I could feel my heart shatter as desperation began to set in. My dad, Samuel Lowe Jr., had been telling me all week that just like Judah and Jerusalem, all we had to do was show up, and God would handle the rest. I believed with my mind, I absolutely did, but my heart was filled with fear. "Jesus said to him, 'If you can believe, all things are possible to him who believes.' Immediately the father of the child cried out and said with tears, 'Lord, I believe; help my unbelief!'" (Mark 9:23–24). But just like with King Jehoshaphat, if we had not shown up, we would have missed seeing God work. And trust me, it was a sight to see. As the old folks say, "We showed up, and God showed out!"

Nothing could have prepared me for the plaintiff testimonies—that proved our points—and general ineptness of the opposing counsel. You could actually see God working. And then I saw God handle everything. After our lunch recess, neither her father, her father's new wife, or her father's mother showed back up. Opposing counsel stated that she had never had a client fail to return to court in her thirty-five years of practicing law. My attorney had never had that happen in his seventeen years of experience.

The judge then awarded me full custody and denied him all visitation. God not only worked out this particular request for custody but did so in such a way that we need not worry or live in fear of the next request. Praise God! "I have heard of You by the hearing of the ear, but now my eye sees You" (Job 42:5).

When Judah and Jerusalem went to the wilderness, they saw that God had caused this great army to destroy themselves. Each praise given by the choir caused God to set ambushes against their enemies. No one escaped. God not only delivered them in his glorious capacity, he did so in a way that rewarded their belief with both spiritual and physical treasures.

There's no greater benefit to a relationship than when trust has been established. God told them that this was his battle and that they would not have to fight. And surprise, surprise, he did exactly what he said. Our King is faithful and steadfast. "God is not a man, so he does not lie. He is not human, so he does not change his mind. Has he ever spoken and failed to act? Has he ever promised and not carried it through?" (Num 23:19 NLT). God delivered me, and my relationship with him since the beginning of this ordeal is more amazing than I ever thought possible. He is allowing me to understand his word and apply it in real ways to my life. My King is allowing me to thirst for his word and crave a more intimate relationship with him. I can only imagine how their trial and deliverance helped to rejuvenate and propel Judah and Jerusalem's desire for God.

In addition to spiritual benefits, Jehoshaphat's kingdom reaped the benefits of the spoils of victory. "When Jehoshaphat and his people came to take away their spoil, they found among them an abundance of valuables on the dead bodies, and precious jewelry, which they stripped off for themselves, more than they could carry away; and they were three days gathering the spoil because there was so much" (2 Chron 20:25).

"Then they returned, every man of Judah and Jerusalem, with Jehoshaphat in front of them, to go back to Jerusalem with joy, for the LORD had made them rejoice over their enemies" (2 Chron 20:27). My once tense house, that had been filled with three stressed adults treading lightly around the huge, custody elephant in the room; too many awful video calls to count; constant interruptions and disrespectful and sometimes bizarre text messages, is now filled with freedom, praise, and gratitude. I never want to forget the sound of the judge's voice when she rendered her decision or the look on my parents' faces as we danced out of the courtroom or the feel of my daughter's hug when I returned home.

For the month prior to the court date, my daughter kept saying, "I stay with you forever." She would practically bring me to tears each time, because I knew there was a possibility that she would be forced away, against both of our wills. I can not even articulate how awesome it felt to finally be able to tell her that yes, she would be with me forever. Praise God!

"Sing to the Lord, all you godly ones! Praise his holy name. For his anger lasts only a moment, but his favor lasts a lifetime! Weeping may last through the night, but joy comes with the morning. You have turned my mourning into joyful dancing. You have taken away my clothes of mourning and clothed me with joy, that I might sing praises to you and not be silent. O Lord my God, I will give you thanks forever!" (Ps 30:4–12 NLT).

Real Life

I LOST SEVEN pounds during the week of my four-day liquid fast
to prepare for court, taking my weight loss to thirty-two pounds
total. Let the record show that I was no longer considered to be
obese. Unfortunately, the following week, my scale informed me
that I was five pounds heavier. Normally, this gain would have
been detrimental to my ego and drive, but not this time. This time
the good Lord equipped me with more knowledge and an under-
standing of how my body responds to IF. Of course, I lost lots of
weight; I doubt I took in 2,000 calories the entire week. That's not
healthy, and that's not what IF is about. It's exactly why I gained
the weight back the following week when my eating returned to
my new IF normal.

The entire week was a real struggle for me, physically. The
Lord had to carry me through each day of my 12,000 steps. It was
unbearably hot, and I was getting tired faster than before. Walking
was more of a task, and it seemed as if it took ten steps to get one. I
was achy and sluggish and miserable. But each day, with the Lord's
help, I fought for and reached my step goal.

I was also much hungrier. I found myself watching the clock
more than usual. There were a few days that I had to physically
leave the house to make sure I didn't end my fasting period prema-
turely. "Therefore, my beloved, flee from idolatry" (1 Cor 10:14).
Simply put, I was a hot mess.

That week really tested my resolve. Normally, that would have
been the beginning of the end for me. Historically, I would have
slacked off with my physical activity and rationalized eating in

ways that were contrary to my goal. Finally, I would have stopped everything, all together. But that's not me anymore, and it's not you either. "Therefore, if anyone is in Christ, he is a new creation; old things have passed away; behold, all things have become new" (2 Cor 5:17).

Today is currently day 75 for me. I've fasted for 1,511 hours. I've lost thirty-four pounds, and my BMI is 29.5. I am no longer obese, praise God! I look and feel amazing. I am still fighting, and I hope you are, too.

"Be strong and courageous, and do the work. Don't be afraid or discouraged, for the Lord God, my God, is with you. He will not fail you or forsake you" (1 Chron 28:20 NLT). I'm sharing this to let you know that you're not alone in this fight. God is with us, and he will see us through. Some days are harder than others for me. The blisters, the chafing (oh my goodness, the chafing!), the sweat, the nausea, and the commercials with all my favorite, yummy foods make this fight extremely difficult at times. But I'm fighting for my life, my girls' lives, their children's lives, and so on and so forth. What are you fighting for? Write it down and say it out loud!

On those days when you wake up and feel as if you've been hit by a bus, and are already hungry-hungry, don't give up! Tell our King your woes and feelings, and draw your strength from him. If you've already slacked off and possibly gained a few pounds back, keep moving forward. Don't let any disappointment or setback keep you from your best you! In Matt 11:29–30, Jesus tells us to "take My yoke upon you. . . . For My yoke is easy and My burden is light."

Gregory Dickow breaks down this passage so beautifully in his *Fast from Wrong Thinking* devotional. He states:

> Most people don't understand what Jesus meant when He said, "Take my yoke upon you . . ." A yoke is a harness placed upon two oxen. It causes them to plow together. So when one gets weak or overwhelmed, he can continue by being pulled by the other. When we feel weighed

down, we need to remember, we are yoked to Him. Jesus is attached to us and will carry the load for us.[1]

Dickow goes on to state:

> God holds you up and pulls you up when you are weak and overwhelmed. You are one with Him. When you feel weak and burdened, remember that He is carrying you.[2]

What an awesome God we serve!

1. Dickow, *Fast from Wrong Thinking.*
2. Dickow, *Fast from Wrong Thinking.*

Trust

IF YOU ARE like me and are parents to young children, have young children in your family, or work around them, I'm sure you've learned just as much from them as they've learned from you. My youngest daughter is fearless. In most situations, she holds little to no regard for her personal safety. She climbs and jumps off things she shouldn't, runs with under developed coordination without hesitation. She's having a blast, while I'm having mini heart attacks, trying to keep her from killing herself.

She is cautious in very few instances. In those brief moments of her carefulness, she has taught me about trust. Every time she gets to the steps that lead to the deck from the back yard, she puts up her tiny hand for someone to grab and help her up. She doesn't look back, she doesn't wait, she doesn't worry. She just knows that someone will be there to help her. I smile every time she does this—after catching my breath from sprinting over to her.

Matthew 18:2–4 states, "Then Jesus called a little child to Him, set him in the midst of them, and said, 'Assuredly, I say to you, unless you are converted and become as little children, you will by no means enter the kingdom of heaven. Therefore whoever humbles himself as this little child is the greatest in the kingdom of heaven.'"

My daughter is a perfect example of how we are to be in our relationship with our heavenly Father. Trials are inevitable. Life is messy, and our sinful nature makes things complicated and exhausting. Change is constant and can seem unbearable. We experience growing pangs and pruning as we grow in our faith, as well.

Fortunately, we have a God that is gracious, merciful, steadfast, and ever-present. He is always with us, and he cares about every minute detail of our lives. Instead of gritting our teeth, as we narcissistically insist on doing things our way, on our time, we need to seek his assistance and guidance first. In doing so, we can alleviate a lot of our frustration, weariness, and strife.

I imagine God looking at us lovingly in our toddler-like attempts to solve problems beyond our capabilities: messy hands trying to clean away our mistakes, all while making bigger messes; tired bodies carrying loads that are too heavy and leaving a trail of items behind us. I thank God that His patience with me far outweighs my patience with my girls. Many times I find myself pleading for my girls to let me help them, because I know a better way. But God is a way better parent than I. He understands that we are just lowly creatures made of dust, and he graciously loves us in spite of ourselves.

This is why he always gives us a way out of our messes. He never allows our load to crush us physically or spiritually. "No test or temptation that comes your way is beyond the course of what others have had to face. All you need to remember is that God will never let you down; he'll never let you be pushed past your limit; he'll always be there to help you come through it" (1 Cor 10:13 Message).

I have never experienced this more than during my IF journey. At day 113, my weight was 210, BMI was 28.2, I had lost 43.4 pounds, and had accumulated 2283 fasting hours. Each day, I would tell myself that I wasn't going to do the fast that day, that I was going to go ahead and eat. But, with God's help, I remained in my fast state until my eating window began. This has not been easy. There have been weeks where I've gained weight, when hunger pangs were severe and just downright awful.

I will say that I have felt my King's presence consistently throughout this whole journey. He is with me in ways that I never thought possible. The more I let go of my false sense of control, the more I feel him leading me. I am ill-equipped to manage the chaos and turmoil that is my life. Mainly, my incessant need to control and my short-sighted decision-making are the cause of the chaos. Letting go has allowed me to focus on abiding in Christ. He will handle the rest. I trust his leadership, as he is the creator of all things, and he knows all things.

"The LORD is my shepherd; I shall not want. He makes me to lie down in green pastures; He leads me beside the still waters. He restores my soul; He leads me in the paths of righteousness for His name's sake" (Ps 23:1–3).

The Daniel Fast

AT DAY 130, I had lost forty-six pounds, had a 27.4 BMI, weighed 208 pounds, and had accrued 2,553 hours of fasting. I went from a snug size 23 to a comfortable size 12–14 pants. I am equal parts shock, joy, and gratitude. This journey has been amazing. My weight loss success has given me the confidence to get out of my comfort zone in other areas of my life as well. Recently, I participated with members of my church family in a corporate fast, in my first Daniel fast.

During the twenty-one-day Daniel fast, you are to abstain from meat, alcohol, bread, and dairy. This fast originates from when Daniel sought the Lord for answers and guidance after a vision. "My lord, because of the vision my sorrows have overwhelmed me, and I have retained no strength" (Dan 10:16). In order to seek guidance, he fasted. "In those days I, Daniel, was mourning three full weeks. I ate no pleasant food, no meat or wine came into my mouth, nor did I anoint myself at all, till three whole weeks were fulfilled" (Dan 10:2–3).

I do want to note that Daniel didn't set out to fast for twenty-one days. There is no spiritual gold star given upon completion. Daniel fasted for answers, guidance, and comfort. Usually, Daniel's prayers were answered very quickly. This particular time, his answer was sent quickly but was delayed. Daniel 10:12–13 states, "Then he said to me, 'Do not fear, Daniel, for from the first day that you set your heart to understand, and to humble yourself before your God, your words were heard; and I have come because of your words. But the prince of the kingdom of Persia withstood me twenty-one days; and behold, Michael, one of the chief princes, came to help me, for I had been left alone there with the kings of Persia.'"

Participating in this corporate fast was a huge deal for me. I am a true carnivore. A steak entree with a side of chicken and shrimp—please and thank you. I love meat. I will eat vegetables, but they are simply there because I have to eat them. As you can imagine, this fast did not appeal to me at all. I had zero expectations and was sure I would not be able to last the entire twenty-one days.

The first week was brutal. Eating only fruits and vegetables during my four-hour eating window left me feeling depleted and unsatisfied. I was hungry, and I wanted meat. It certainly didn't help that my family ate as normal—grilling and cooking just as before. I was being constantly bombarded with the sights and smells of all the yummies I was craving.

The second week was unbearable. I was hungry-hungry, and a rising layer of severe hangry was quickly approaching. I broke down. Family members helped me to realize that I was doing two fasts at the same time and needed to stop one. During the Daniel fast, participants are permitted to eat during the day. My IF was restricting the Daniel fast, which was adding to my difficulty. I had to stop one.

This is when I came face-to-face with my old nemesis: fear. My instinct was to stop the Daniel fast. No meat, it was a no-brainer. But mainly, I still didn't feel ready to start eating unrestrictedly. I have terrible eating habits, and I know all too well the ease and quickness in which weight is gained. The thought of eating normally was terrifying. My aunt Brenda reminded me that I needed to turn this over to God and trust that he would help me. She reminded me that God is there always and encouraged me to put my hand up and allow him to help me up those steps.

So I let go. I acknowledged my fear and I put up my hand. True to his promise and nature, he was there for me. I ate very timidly for the last week of the Daniel fast. My fear of gorging and eating unhealthily were just that: fears. That's the beauty of a lifestyle change over a diet; it becomes part of you. As my dad says, "We don't fast; we are a fast." We are in a constant state of being in control of our bodies, cravings, and desires. Our heavenly Father is transforming us. "Don't copy the behavior and customs of this world, but let God transform you into a new person by changing the way you think. Then you will learn to know God's will for you, which is good and pleasing and perfect" (Rom 12:2 NLT).

In a million years, I never thought I could go any length of time without meat—certainly not twenty-one days. I never thought I could be free from food at all. I never thought I could be free from obesity and shame, but God has freed me. The knowledge of this freedom and the corresponding gratitude has made it possible for my other shackles to be loosened. God has helped me in my quest of abstinence and celibacy. He is actively freeing me from unforgiveness and secrecy. God's soft voice is quieting the chaos in my heart and mind. He's guiding me with his word through the mess of my life to him. Praise God!

I pray that your IF journey is strengthening your relationship with the one true God. My constant prayer is that you are allowing God to help you tackle your other vices. Whether they be sex, smoking, alcohol, masturbation, marijuana, pain killers, sleeping pills, porn, or drugs, God is the only way to freedom. Titus 2:11–14 states, "For the grace of God that brings salvation has appeared to all men, teaching us that, denying ungodliness and worldly lusts, we should live soberly, righteously, and godly in the present age, looking for the blessed hope and glorious appearing of our great God and Savior Jesus Christ, who gave Himself for us, that He might redeem us from every lawless deed and purify for Himself His own special people, zealous for good works."

The Plateau

My ORIGINAL WEIGHT loss goal was seventy pounds to be lost by November. By the middle of October, it was pretty obvious that I was not going to make it. Although I was a little disappointed, it was not the end of the world. My weight loss had been minimal since July. My scale was constantly changing. One week, I'd lose three pounds; the next week, I'd gain back two. It was pretty frustrating, to say the least.

I was in a plateau. A plateau in your weight loss simply means that the calories you are consuming are equal to the calories you are burning. It boils down to math. You gain weight when you take in more calories than you burn, and you lose weight when you burn more than you ingest.

The Mayo Clinic states the following in their weight loss article entitled "Getting Past a Weight-Loss Plateau":[1]

> During the first few weeks of losing weight, a rapid drop is normal. In part, this is because when you cut calories, the body gets needed energy initially by releasing its stores of glycogen—a type of carbohydrate found in the muscles and liver.
>
> Glycogen is partly made of water, so when glycogen is burned for energy, it releases water. This results in weight loss that's mostly water. This effect is temporary, however.
>
> As you lose weight, you lose some muscle along with fat. Muscle helps to increase the rate at which you burn calories, also known as metabolism. So as you lose weight,

1. Mayo Clinic Staff, "Getting Past."

your metabolism declines, causing you to burn fewer calories than you did at your heavier weight.

Your slower metabolism will slow your weight loss, even if you eat the same number of calories that helped you lose weight. When the calories you burn equal the calories you eat, you reach a plateau.

If you've plateaued keep pushing forward. You're not alone. Those who took this weight loss journey before you and those who will journey after you have and will experience the same frustration. It can be debilitating to think of more ways to restrict yourself, especially when you're already giving one hundred percent for minimal results. Allow yourself to feel the aggravation, but don't linger there.

Focus on why you started this journey in the first place. Let your initial reasoning pull you down from the plateau and back to the plush grass of weight loss. Get back to the basics and really assess your food intake and daily activity. This journey is an accountability mirror from which you cannot hide. Your body, clothes, and the scale will not allow you to lie to yourself. For that, I am truly thankful.

I think my goal of seventy pounds in five months may have been a bit too ambitious. I also made reaching my 12,000 daily steps less of a priority, and I'm sure this was the main reason for my plateau. For the last month, I was averaging only between 7,000 and 9,000 daily steps. To be honest, I had zero idea how I was going to manage fitting in all my steps with added daily responsibilities and less daylight. I felt overwhelmed every time I tried to strategized and just ended up doing nothing.

Dr. Michael Youssef said it best in his "Dangers of Small Compromises" devotional:[2]

> In the book of Judges, we see the Israelites didn't take God seriously when He warned against the moral and spiritual pollution of the Canaanites and their idols. The Israelites mingled with them, traded with them,

2. Youssef, "Judges: Choosing God's Way."

sometimes enslaved them, and eventually began to intermarry with them and worship pagan idols with them. The Israelites set themselves up for decline and collapse when they failed to obey God's commandments. They settled for half a victory.

Before we judge the Israelites too harshly, we need to examine ourselves and ask: Have we settled for half a victory over our sin and self-defeating habits? Have we driven out our bad habits of gluttony, gossip, lust, bitterness, anger, foul language, or addiction? Do we excuse our vices or are we committed to complete victory over them by driving them out of our lives? These "small" compromises (at least we like to think of them as small) are an accommodation with the enemy. We are symbolically mingling and intermarrying with the Canaanites— and if we do not drive them out, we will end up defeated.

That was a wake-up call. I was definitely settling for a half victory. I was completely content to rest on the weight I lost already. But that would have been a half victory. This compromise in my commitment to conquering my issues with food would later be my downfall, just as it had always been in the past. Tell your bad habits: enough! I don't want anything to hinder my relationship with Christ, and I know that you don't either.

The next day I was determined to reach my step goal, and I did. It was amazing. Being out in nature with God again, walking and meditating on him and his word was just what I needed, spiritually, mentally, and emotionally. It's the middle of October, and fall is in full swing. The leaves are turning colors, the wind is blowing in cool air, and the birds are extra active. God's artistic magnificence makes it almost impossible not to praise him. "Worthy are You, our Lord and God, to receive the glory and the honor and the power; for You created all things, and because of Your will they exist, and were created and brought into being" (Rev 4:11 AMP).

I also became more aware of what I was consuming during my eating window. We become creatures of habit so quickly. I feel like I have the same day everyday. Our activities and movements become second nature. We do things and don't even realize it. Try to stay in the moment, and really be aware of what and how much you're putting into your body. Ask yourself if you are hungry, or do you just want to eat? Asking myself this really helps me take stock of why I'm eating.

Below are other tricks that you may find helpful in keeping you from eating just for the sake of eating.

- Drink a bottle of water before each meal

- Use smaller plates and bowls.

- Brush your teeth or rinse with mouthwash after each meal. There's no point in overindulging if it doesn't taste right.

- Don't buy your guilty pleasure snacks. You can not eat what's not there.

- Remember that your cravings will pass. Stay strong.

- Keep careful track of your sugar intake. According to the American Heart Association (AHA), men should have no more than 37.5 grams of sugar each day, and women should have no more than 25 grams. Be vigilant; there is sugar and added sugars in everything.

- Turn off the television. Commercials are constantly bombarding you with food advertisements. There are 5 million cooking and baking shows, and every one that I've ever seen makes me hungry.

- The next time you get the urge to snack unnecessarily, open your Bible. Take your mind off of yourself and read God's word. "So letting your sinful nature control your mind leads to death. But letting the Spirit control your mind leads to life andpeace" (Rom 8:6 NLT).

I am not letting go of my weight loss goal. I have accepted that it will take longer than expected, and I'm 100% OK with that. Stay in your battle. We can conquer this enemy with our God's guidance. "I am the Lord, the God of all the peoples of the world. Is anything too hard for me?" (Jer 32:27 NLT).

Game Changer

TODAY I REQUESTED time to walk two of my laps around the neighborhood—3,000 steps—kid-free. I was able to walk one and a half laps without being accosted by my girls. I gave in to their requests of "up, mama" and "carry me." I begrudgingly abandoned my walking efforts and began to carry them both back to the house. I understood that by doing this, I would not reach my step goal for yet another day. I was halfway back to the house when a small voice from within screamed no!

I was not going to let my step goal go so easily. I was going to fight for what I needed to do, for me. I was not asking for a weekend away by myself or running off for a week alone. I just needed twenty minutes to take care of me. I do not know about you, but I have the hardest time feeling like I should take care of my needs. Since having my girls, my second daughter especially, I feel completely invisible and unimportant. I am basically a vending machine/jungle gym hybrid. This is where my mother would say, "You should have thought of this before you had kids." I love being a mom, and I adore my girls. Their needs come first, and I would not have it any other way. But twenty minutes is not a lot to ask. I think I have earned at least that.

I carried my girls against all odds for the remainder of my walk. My girls together weigh nearly sixty pounds. That is squirming, nose-to-nose touching, neck rubbing, swaying back and forth, sixty pounds. I even walked extra. I made it to over 13,000 total steps that day. I felt so empowered and validated. My God gave me the strength to carry them. I was able to carry them all the way back to the driveway before my arms gave out. "He gives strength to the weary, and to him who has no might He increases power" (Isa 40:29 AMP).

I cannot lose the remaining twenty-four pounds in my own strength. That's why I have always failed in the past. It's the same reason why you've never been able to lose weight and keep it off. We're relying on ourselves, and it won't work.

Our flesh is too strong and too powerful. That's why our fasting is so important. The only way to weaken the flesh's hold is to deny its desires and strengthen our spirit with things of the Lord. Our spirit is the only thing that can defeat and bring our flesh into submission. But the spirit must be strong enough to battle with the flesh. The spirit needs God's Word and obedience. Galatians 5:16–17 (NLT) tells us, "So I say, let the Holy Spirit guide your lives. Then you won't be doing what your sinful nature craves. The sinful nature wants to do evil, which is just the opposite of what the Spirit wants. And the Spirit gives us desires that are the opposite of what the sinful nature desires. These two forces are constantly fighting each other, so you are not free to carry out your good intentions."

Getting healthy and staying healthy is an uphill battle. It would be easy to give up and indulge the unhealthy habits that have wreaked havoc on our bodies and self-esteem. It's exhausting having to fight every day, all day. Just remember, "Do not be afraid nor dismayed . . . , for the battle is not yours, but God's" (2 Chron 20:15).

Man Down

My scale has informed me that I gained twelve pounds. I was absolutely devastated and completely disgusted. Each morning for the past week, I was a pound heavier. When I saw 220, my heart broke.

It was a rough day. I wish I could tell you that I met this setback with grace and dignity, immersing myself in God's Word for strength and encouragement. But that did not happen. I comforted myself with sugar-free ice cream and sour cream and onion chips. I indulged in self-pity, shame, and seclusion. Unlike before, this all just made me feel worse.

I had been struggling with my sweet tooth and my desires for unhealthy foods. If I'm being honest, I hadn't been doing a particularly good job resisting and had indulged more than I should. Even though the Lord has freed me from the powers that food has over me, in my sin and fleshly state I still desire aspects of my unhealthy lifestyle. I see now that I was trying to get back to Egypt.

My pastor would say, "There is no going back to Egypt. Once God frees you, you're freed." When God freed the Israelites from slavery under Pharaoh, he took them through the desert and met their physical needs by providing water and food—manna or "bread from heaven." "Now the manna was like coriander seed, and its color like the color of bdellium. The people went about and gathered it, ground it on millstones or beat it in the mortar, cooked it in pans, and made cakes of it; and its taste was like the taste of pastry prepared with oil. And when the dew fell on the camp in the night, the manna fell on it" (Num 11:7–9).

Amazing, right? The manna was nutritionally perfect, giving the Israelites all they would need to survive. With that being said, it is never stated that the manna was tasty. I liken it to a protein and vitamin-packed rice cake, but that is just my opinion. I'm sure in its powerful simplicity, the manna left the Israelites longing for more, craving more. They too were only human. Too many times, I have eaten as I should and just simply wanted something else, even though I was no longer hungry. I can absolutely identify with the Israelites in their constant complaints to Moses.

Numbers 11:4–6 states, "Now the mixed multitude who were among them yielded to intense craving; so the children of Israel also wept again and said: 'Who will give us meat to eat? We remember the fish which we ate freely in Egypt, the cucumbers, the melons, the leeks, the onions, and the garlic; but now our whole being is dried up; there is nothing at all except this manna before our eyes!'"

Brian Leung, in the comments section of an online article I once read, perfectly explains the Israelites' behavior. He states:

> The Israelites were slaves, in bondage under the Egyptian Pharaoh. They were suffering under their bondage, and it was time for Moses to lead them out of Egypt and slavery, as detailed in Exodus.
>
> God performed many miracles to compel Pharaoh to let the Israelites go. It took ten plagues before Pharaoh allowed them to leave. When the Israelites were finally freed, they wandered in the desert, with the assurance from the Lord through Moses that they would arrive at the Promised Land. However, during their journey, the Israelites began to miss life in the big city. Despite being under bondage, they had grown accustomed to Egyptian life. Many of them also engaged in the idolatry of the Egyptian culture. Some of them returned to committing idolatry, which made the Lord wroth.
>
> The fact that many of the Israelites wanted to return to Egypt is a testament of the fact that as people, we often have doubts and are of little faith. We doubt our own

abilities, but we also, at times, doubt God's ability and His promise to us.

The Israelites didn't want to do the hard work of travelling through the desert. They wanted what they knew and were accustomed to. They feared the unknown and had little faith in the Lord.

Does this sound like you?—because it screams Carol. I am accustomed to my unhealthy lifestyle. I am accustomed to being morbidly obese. That's easy. My new, smaller clothes, family, and even this book hold me to a level of accountability with my weight that is unfamiliar and new. This new accountability is uncomfortable, restrictive, and, at times, stifling. It reminds me of the cast I had as a child when I broke my arm roller skating. I didn't like the cast; it itched incessantly and became annoying almost immediately. The cast immobilized my arm so it could heal properly. Just like this lifestyle of IF, the restrictions are allowing my body and mind to heal from the damage of gluttony. This is not about simply losing weight. It's about drawing closer to God and allowing him to lead us to his will and desires. His will is the promise land of our freedom.

More so than the restrictions and cravings is the ever-present fear that I will not be able to reach my goal. If I reach my goal, fear is telling me that I will not be able to maintain my healthy lifestyle. I'm self-sabotaging.

Lisa Jeffs, renowned life coach, states in her article "Self-Sabotaging Behavior and Thoughts":[1]

> Self-sabotage is when we actively or passively take steps to prevent ourselves from reaching our goals. This behavior can affect nearly every aspect of life—be it a relationship, a career goal, or a personal goal, such as weight loss. Although quite common, it is an incredibly frustrating cycle of behavior that lowers our self-confidence and leaves us feeling stuck.

1. Jeffs, "Self-Sabotaging Behavior and Thoughts."

Paul talks about this stuck feeling. He understood all too well the cycle of self-sabotage and its link to our sinful, fallen nature. In Rom 7:18–20 (NIV), Paul says, "For I know that good itself does not dwell in me, that is, in my sinful nature. For I have the desire to do what is good, but I cannot carry it out. For I do not do the good I want to do, but the evil I do not want to do—this I keep on doing. Now if I do what I do not want to do, it is no longer I who does it, but it is sin living in me that does it." This is why we all struggle to do the right things and make the right choices. This applies to every aspect of our lives, whether it be eating healthily, building or repairing relationships, and dealing with all forms of addiction. I want to eat healthily, be healthy, be patient and long-suffering, but I struggle constantly and fail more times than I'd like to admit.

Through this journey, God has allowed me to understand that it's not about my failures at all. I'm going to have failures and setbacks. So are you, and that's OK. It's about getting up, starting over, and readjusting. In our failures, we reach a level of humility that we seldom reach from the mountaintops of success. We tend to humbly reach out to our Creator for guidance in the midst of our failures. This is where he graciously picks us up, reassures, and corrects us. God knows all too well that we are just lowly creatures made of dirt, with more limitations than anything.

After all, God made us to show the devil and other fallen angels that he could create an inferior creature that would freely serve, love, worship him, and carry out his will. God knows we are basically useless, but with him, there are no limitations as to what we can accomplish in our lives, families, and communities. "For I know the thoughts that I think toward you, says the LORD, thoughts of peace and not of evil, to give you a future and a hope. Then you will call upon Me and go and pray to Me, and I will listen to you. And you will seek Me and find Me when you search for Me with all your heart. I will be found by you, says the LORD, and I will bring you back from your captivity" (Jer 29:11–14).

Hope

"Being confident of this very thing, that He who has begun a good work in you will complete it until the day of Jesus Christ." Philippians 1:6

In line only behind Scriptures about salvation, Phil 1:6 is one of the most beautiful and hopeful Scriptures I know. I take comfort in my position as a work in progress. We know that nothing good comes from ourselves but of God. We're in this fight and on this journey because of him. He will finish what he started, in spite of us. Thank God!

Since the gain, I have been readjusting everything related to my IF journey. I have changed my fasting window, where I walk, my daily step count, and my portion sizes. I'm not at my goal weight yet, but the numbers are going in the right direction; I'm no longer gaining weight. The first two pounds lost since the gain were probably my favorite pounds ever lost. I have learned to never be too proud to celebrate the small victories. I celebrated those pounds, and I thanked God for seeing me to those pounds. I know there will be many more pounds lost as I reach my goal weight and many more celebrations. Now more than ever, I believe wholeheartedly that I will reach my goal.

This weight gain wasn't all bad, though. It was actually quite rejuvenating. The gain gave me a renewed sense of commitment to not only IF but my reasons behind this journey: strengthening my relationship with Christ, learning his will, breaking negative familial patterns for my girls, and being healthy. We so easily get sidetracked from our reasons to get healthy and focus only on dropping pounds and what the scale says. Recently, I've had to take the scale out of my bedroom. I was weighing myself all day, every day, and I was becoming obsessed with the numbers. It was driving me crazy. Though it is good to track your progress, fixating on anything in the process is counterproductive. The Lord allowed me to see the error of my ways and led me back to a good place mentally and emotionally. Being in a better place allowed me to refocus on my goals.

Whatever your goals are, stay the course. Do not stop, and don't give up. There's a reason you're alive, there's a reason you're fighting for your health, there's a reason for your pain, and there's a reason you're reading this right now. Dig deep into God's word for all your desire—both physically and spiritually. Stick close to the Creator, and seek his will and kingdom agenda. Colossians 3:2 (AMP) states, "Set your mind and keep focused habitually on the things above [the heavenly things], not on things that are on the earth [which have only temporal value]."

Now that we understand the connection between the body and soul and the physical and spiritual, this fight for health is even more dire. I hope you can see that our bodies and health are under attack. Excess sugar in everything, ridiculously large portion sizes, and overly fatty foods are keeping the population as a whole overweight, sick, distracted, and exhausted. We cannot be used to advance God's kingdom if we are too sickly to work and too large to move. As his church and soldiers in this battle against Satan and his minions, we need to be healthy enough to fight. "A final word: Be strong in the Lord and in his mighty power. Put on all of God's armor so that you will be able to stand firm against all strategies of the devil. For we are not fighting against flesh-and-blood enemies, but against evil rulers and authorities of the unseen world, against mighty powers in this dark world, and against evil spirits in the heavenly places. Therefore, put on every piece of God's armor so you will be able to resist the enemy in the time of evil. Then after the battle you will still be standing firm. Stand your ground, putting on the belt of truth and the body armor of God's righteous-ness. For shoes, put on the peace that comes from the Good News so that you will be fully prepared. In addition to all of these, hold up the shield of faith to stop the fiery arrows of the devil. Put on salvation as your helmet, and take the sword of the Spirit, which is the word of God" (Eph 6:10–17 NLT).

My IF experience has completely changed my life for the better. I hope that my journey has motivated and inspired you toward a healthier lifestyle. My prayer is that you do whatever it takes to start and stay both physically and spiritually healthy. Keep pushing! You can do this! Do not give up! "Therefore, since we are surrounded by such a huge crowd of witnesses to the life of faith, let us strip off every weight that slows us down, especially the sin that so easily trips us up. And let us run with endurance the race God has set before us. We do this by keeping our eyes on Jesus, the champion who initiates and perfects our faith. Because of the joy awaiting him, he endured the cross, disregarding its shame. Now he is seated in the place of honor beside God's throne. Think of all the hostility he endured from sinful people; then you won't become weary and give up" (Heb 12:1–3 NLT).

Bibliography

Centers for Disease Control and Prevention. "Defining Adult Overweight and Obesity." https://www.cdc.gov/obesity/adult/defining.html.

"Counting Your Steps." https://www.10000steps.org.au/articles/counting-steps/.

Dickow, Gregory. *Fast from Wrong Thinking: Forty-Day Devotional.* In *YouVersion Bible App: Daily Study, Audio and Prayer.* Edmond, OK: Life.Church, 2008, 2021. Mobile App 9.0.6.

Fastic: Fasting App and Intermittent Fasting Tracker. Berlin: Fastic GmbH & Co. KG, 2020. Mobile app 1.21.0. https://play.google.com/store/apps/details?id=de.fastic.app&hl=en_US&gl=US.

Galvin, Gaby. "The US Obesity Rate Now Tops Forty Percent." Feb. 2, 2020. https://www.usnews.com/news/healthiest-communities/articles/2020-02-27/us-obesity-rate-passes-40-percent.

Jeffs, Lisa. "Self-Sabotaging Behavior and Thoughts: What Causes It and How to Rise Above It." Sept. 30, 2018. https://lisajeffs.com/en-us/self-sabotaging-behavior-thoughts-what-causes-it-and-how-to-rise-above-it/.

Mayo Clinic Staff. "Getting Past a Weight-Loss Plateau." https://www.mayoclinic.org/healthy-lifestyle/weight-loss/in-depth/weight-loss-plateau/art-20044615.

Youssef, Michael. "Judges: Choosing God's Way, Day 2: The Dangers of Small Compromises." In *YouVersion Bible App: Daily Study, Audio and Prayer.* Edmond, OK: Life.Church, 2008, 2021. Mobile App 9.0.6.

www.ingramcontent.com/pod-product-compliance
Lightning Source LLC
Chambersburg PA
CBHW051009060726
47593CB00017B/1271